DATE NIGHT
COOKBOOK

DATE NIGHT COOKBOOK

Summersdale Publishers Ltd
46 West Street
Chichester
West Sussex
PO19 1RP
UK

www.summersdale.com

Printed and bound in Croatia

ISBN: 978-1-84953-871-8

Substantial discounts on bulk quantities of Summersdale books are available to corporations, professional associations and other organisations. For details contact general enquiries: telephone: +44 (0) 1243 771107 or email: enquiries@summersdale.com.

DATE NIGHT COOKBOOK

Rebecca Warbis

summersdale

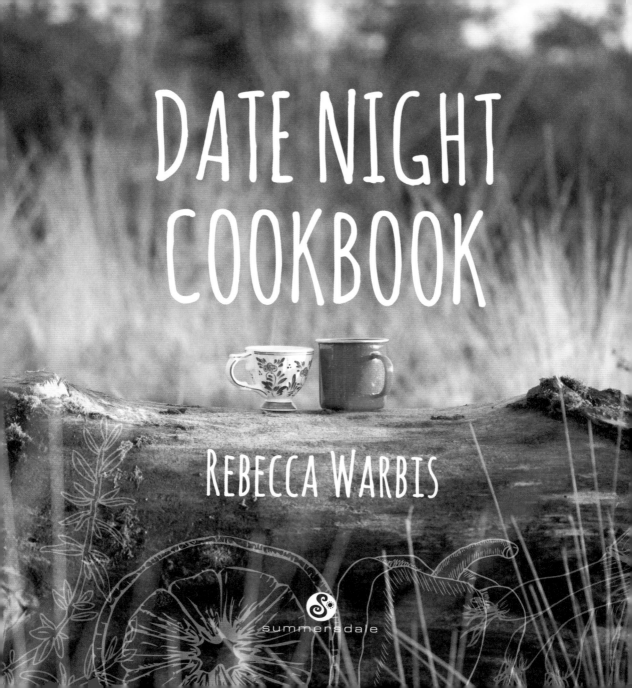

*To my family, friends and boyfriend –
Thanks for everything!*

CONTENTS

- Chapter Seven -
DINING IN PARIS

- Chapter Eight -
MOVIE MARATHON

- Chapter Nine -
UNDER THE STARS

- Chapter One -
Indoor Tent Night

A great date for a special evening, whether
it's the initial 'Where are we at?' chat
or even if it's a proposal on the cards,
this date night has got you covered!

Fondue to Share

Time: 15 minutes

350 g Cheddar cheese
100 g mozzarella
145 ml milk
pinch dry mustard
pinch nutmeg
1 clove garlic
1 large loaf bread, pretzels
or breadsticks to serve

1. Grate both cheeses and add to a saucepan on the hob, melting gently.

2. Stir continuously, slowly adding the milk.

3. Increase the heat by half again and, when the mixture is bubbling, stir in the dry mustard and nutmeg.

4. Keep stirring until the fondue is thick and creamy.

5. Halve the garlic clove and rub it around the inside of the fondue pan. This flavours the cheese really well!

6. Light the fondue candle, and, when the pot is warm, add the mixture.

7. Serve with bread cubes, pretzels or breadsticks for dipping.

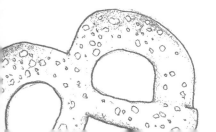

Campfire Potato Bowls

Time: 1 hour 20 minutes

2 large baking potatoes
4 eggs
2 rashers bacon
1 tbsp butter
4 cherry tomatoes
handful pine nuts
1 tbsp fresh parsley
salt and pepper

1. Preheat the oven to 200°C (gas mark 6) and pierce the potatoes all over. Cook for one hour on a greased baking tray.

2. When cooked, the potatoes will be soft and slightly squishy. Leave to cool.

3. Halve both potatoes then scoop out the middles, leaving the edges around 1 cm thick. Try not to break the skin.

4. Crack the eggs one by one into a pouring jug, pouring the yolk and enough white to fill each potato to the brim.

5. Fry the bacon in the butter, then slice and scatter over the top of each potato half with sliced tomato, pine nuts and parsley, then season with salt and pepper.

6. Bake at 180°C (gas mark 4) until the eggs are cooked.

After-Dinner S'mores

Time: 15 minutes

12 pink and white marshmallows
12 Rich Tea biscuits
6 squares of chocolate

1. Thread the marshmallows on to skewers and toast them over a fondue flame.

2. Sandwich two marshmallows between two biscuits. Repeat until all your ingredients are used up.

3. Melt the chocolate in the microwave or on the hob then drizzle a big scoop over each s'more.

BE YOUR OWN KIND
OF BEAUTIFUL

– Chapter Two –
BREAKFAST IN BED

A great lazy date for those days off.
Rain or shine, nothing beats a day in
bed with these great recipes.

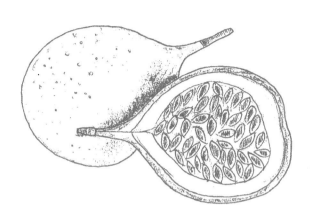

Lazy Breakfast Smoothie

Time: 10 minutes

300 g fresh mango
1 tbsp honey
250 ml milk
200 g fat-free yogurt
1 orange, halved
2 passion fruit, halved
Seed mix to top

1. Chop the mango into small pieces and blend with the honey, milk and yogurt in a blender for three minutes on a medium speed.

2. Squeeze the orange and add the juice to the mixture, blending as you go. The ideal consistency is smooth and yogurt-like.

3. Scoop out and stir in the passion fruit pulp, and sprinkle the seeds over the top. I always opt for sunflower seeds. Yum!

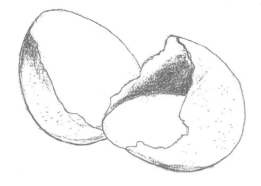

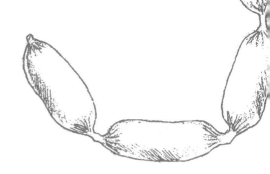

ENGLISH BREAKFAST IN BED

Time: 40 minutes

4–6 sausages
4–6 bacon rashers
250 g vine tomatoes
1 tbsp olive oil, plus extra
to coat backing tray
4 eggs
bread
wholegrain mustard to serve
salt and pepper to serve

1. Preheat the oven to 200°C (gas mark 6).

2. Coat a baking tray in oil, then spread the sausages out, making sure they're evenly coated in oil.

3. Add the bacon and place in the preheated oven for 15 minutes until everything is light brown, turning occasionally.

4. Place the tomatoes on to the tray with another drizzle of oil.

5. Return to the oven for about seven minutes and then remove and leave to the side.

6. Take a frying pan and warm the oil.

7. Crack and fry the eggs in the pan, and when the whites are set, toast the bread.

8. Serve with some wholegrain mustard and a sprinkle of salt and pepper, and enjoy!

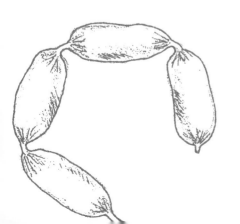

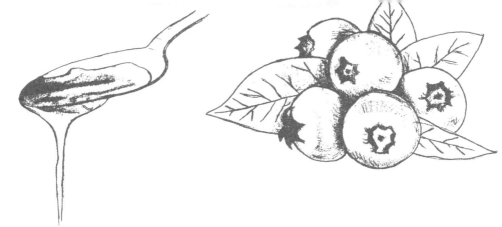

Under-The-Covers Pancakes

Time: 25 minutes

300 g self-raising flour
1 tbsp caster sugar
2 medium eggs
1 tsp vanilla extract
300 ml milk
1 tbsp butter
200 g blueberries
honey to serve

1. Sieve the flour and sugar into a large bowl.

2. Break in the eggs, then pour in the vanilla extract and milk. Blend with a whisk until smooth.

3. Melt the butter in a non-stick frying pan and spoon in a small amount of the mixture, letting it form into a circle.

4. On a high heat, cook until the edges start to solidify then flip with a spatula and brown the other side.

5. Make as many as the mixture allows and keep the finished pancakes in the oven on a very low heat for warmth.

6. Warm the blueberries in the microwave and scatter over your pancakes, along with as much honey as you like!

Talking to you makes my day

- Chapter Three -

Picnic Date

Heathlands, forests or close to home,
wherever this date takes you, these ideas
will make your picnic date truly memorable.

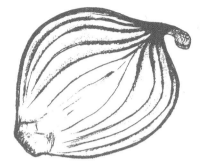

FETA SALAD

Time: 20 minutes

1 aubergine
1 red onion
50 g pine nuts
200 g rocket
100 g feta cheese
1 tbsp balsamic vinegar
1 tbsp olive oil
pinch of pepper

1. Slice the aubergine lengthways into ½-cm-wide strips.

2. Brush each slice with oil, then fry in a pan until browned and cooked through and leave to cool.

3. Cut the onion into slices and gently fry in oil until soft, but not caramelised.

4. In a dry frying pan (using no oil) toast the pine nuts until golden.

5. Place several slices of aubergine on each plate.

6. Scatter a handful of rocket leaves on top.

7. Sprinkle the nuts and onion over the rocket.

8. Top with crumbled feta.

9. Mix together the balsamic vinegar, pepper and oil in a mug, and drizzle over the salad.

Frittata to Share

Time: 50 minutes

3–4 potatoes, preferably Maris Pipers
2 onions
7–8 eggs, enough to cover the potato
salt and pepper
½ bag of spinach

1. Spread oil all around the bottom of a frying pan to cover.

2. Chop the potatoes into enough 2-cm cubes to cover the bottom of the pan.

3. Slowly fry the cubes in the oil on a low-to-medium heat and keep turning them until they are golden brown. Keep them moving with lots of oil to stop them burning.

4. Slice onions thinly and add to the pan. Cook for a further 5–10 minutes.

5. Beat the eggs in a bowl, adding salt, pepper and the spinach, chopped finely.

6. Pour the eggs in the pan and, on a low to medium heat, cook for about 15–20 minutes.

7. Grill the top, until the eggs are cooked, and turn upside down on to a plate. *Voilà*!

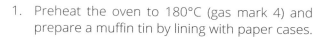

BLUEBERRY MUFFIN INFATUATION

Time: 50 minutes

270 g plain flour
2 tsp baking powder
200 g blueberries
120 g unsalted butter
250 g caster sugar
2 eggs
130 ml milk
1 tsp vanilla extract
1 lemon, halved
handful of sugar crystals
50 g white chocolate

1. Preheat the oven to 180°C (gas mark 4) and prepare a muffin tin by lining with paper cases.

2. Grab a medium-sized bowl and sieve the flour and baking powder together. Add the blueberries and leave to the side.

3. In a separate bowl, mix together the butter and sugar. Whisk in the eggs, milk and vanilla extract until a thick batter is formed.

4. Then, a spoonful at a time, stir in the dry mixture and beat until smooth. Add a big squeeze of lemon.

5. When mixed together, transfer 3 tbsp of mixture into each case then cook for 30 minutes until golden brown.

6. When cool, sprinkle with sugar crystals and drizzle with melted white chocolate. Enjoy!

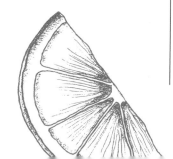

IN YOU,
I'VE FOUND
MY CLOSEST,
TRUEST FRIEND

– Chapter Four –
Dusk Beach Date

Take candles, blankets and a BBQ
and experience total escapism
with this dusk beach date night.

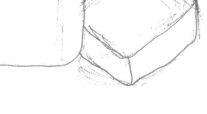

Raspberry Companion

Time: 10 minutes

50 ml gin
12 raspberries
100 g ice
2 tsp sugar
1 bottle sparkling
wine or Prosecco
2 sprigs thyme

1. Pour around 25 ml gin into each cocktail glass.

2. With your fingers, break up around six raspberries per person and add to your glasses.

3. Add ice and 1 tsp of sugar to each glass, stirring until mixed.

4. Fill to the brim with Prosecco (or something fizzy) and finish off with a sprig of thyme in each glass.

COUPLE'S KEBABS

Time: 10 minutes

3 chicken breasts
1 red pepper
10 small mushrooms
10 cherry tomatoes
100 ml clear honey
50 ml olive oil
several squeezes lime
salt and pepper
chilli flakes

1. Chop the chicken and pepper into chunks and thread them on to metal kebab skewers, alternating with the mushrooms and tomatoes.

2. Cook on the BBQ for ten minutes each side or until the chicken is golden brown and well cooked.

3. When they look ready, rotate the kebabs over a plate while drizzling honey and oil.

4. Finally top your kebabs with the lime, salt, pepper and chilli flakes and nibble away!

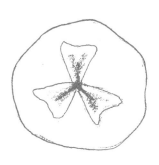

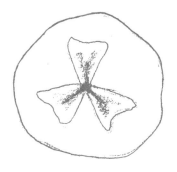

BEACH BAKED BANANAS

Time: 20 minutes

4 bananas
1 tbsp sugar
4 tbsp honey
1 tsp vanilla extract
50 g of pecans, lightly crushed
yogurt or cream to serve

1. Take four pieces of foil around 30 cm by 30 cm and set aside.

2. Slice each banana straight down the middle. Sprinkle with sugar, honey, vanilla extract and pecans, and then tightly wrap each banana in a piece of foil.

3. Place on the BBQ, turning occasionally, until the fruit has softened and the outer skin has mostly blackened. To check this you'll have to partly unwrap each pack, so be really careful as they get super hot.

4. Serve with yogurt or a naughty helping of cream.

I WANT TO
HAVE ADVENTURES
WITH YOU!

– Chapter Five –
Afternoon Tea

Make this a truly British date with a
great mix of sweet and savoury treats,
along with lots of cups of tea!

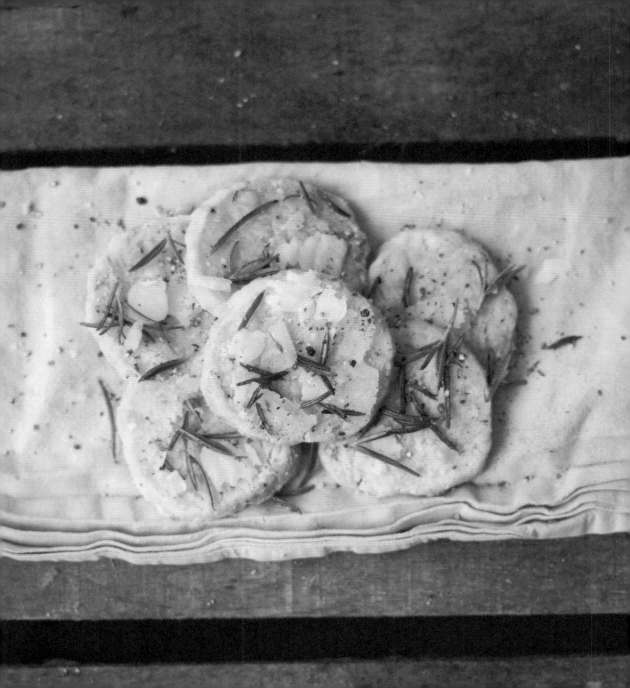

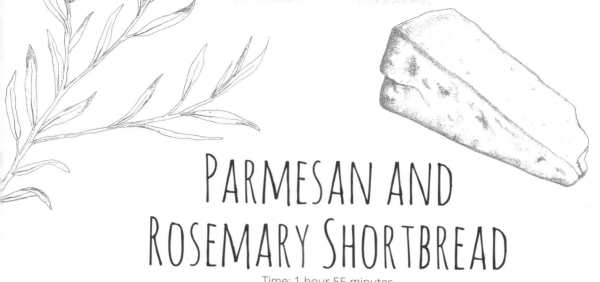

PARMESAN AND ROSEMARY SHORTBREAD

Time: 1 hour 55 minutes

160 g plain flour
110 g butter
2 egg yolks
100 g grated Parmesan
salt and pepper
fresh rosemary
flaked Parmesan, to serve

1. Sieve the flour into a bowl. Add the butter and rub with the flour until it resembles breadcrumbs.

2. When combined add the yolks, Parmesan, salt and pepper and mix together until smooth.

3. Knead to form a stiff, smooth dough. Then make your dough into a long rolling-pin shape and cover with cling film. This then needs to be left in the fridge for around one hour.

4. Preheat the oven to 180°C (gas mark 4).

5. Grease up a baking tray with oil and slice your dough into 1-cm-thick circles.

6. Cook for 20–25 minutes and remove when the dough starts to brown.

7. Fry the rosemary in oil until browned and top the shortbread with this and Parmesan flakes.

English Beef and Mustard Sandwiches

Time: 15 minutes

1 red onion
1 loaf seeded brown bread
2 tbsp wholegrain mustard
handful watercress or rocket
6 thin slices cooked beef

1. Thinly slice the onion and fry in oil until browned.

2. Thickly slice the loaf and then spread heavily with wholegrain mustard.

3. Load each sandwich with a large helping of your chosen salad, fried onions and beef.

4. When all of the filling is packed in, carefully slice the large sandwich with a sharp knife into quarters, making smaller snack-like sandwiches.

English Scones with Jam and Cream

Time: 35 minutes

350 g self-raising flour
1 tsp baking powder
85 g butter
4 tbsp caster sugar
180 ml milk
1 tsp lemon juice
1 tsp vanilla extract
clotted cream to serve
jam to serve

1. Preheat the oven to 220°C (gas mark 7) and grease a baking tray with butter.

2. Sieve the flour and baking powder into a bowl and then combine with the butter, making it into breadcrumbs.

3. Mix in the sugar. Then slowly add milk, lemon juice and vanilla extract and knead into a 1.5-cm-thick dough.

4. Cover the tabletop in flour when rolling out to stop the dough from sticking and cut into round scone shapes. Lay on the baking tray with around a 4-cm gap between each one.

5. Bake for 10 minutes until they are a golden brown colour and serve with clotted cream and jam!

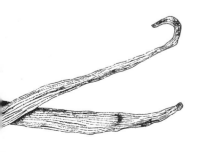

COLLECT MOMENTS, NOT THINGS!

– Chapter Six –

All Dressed Up, Nowhere to Go

Enjoy five-star dining without leaving your house This date night is one way to make a really great impression or to ask that very special question! *Bon appétit, mes amis.*

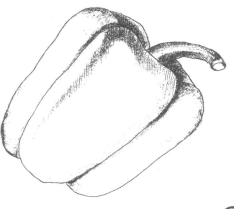

CHARGRILLED VEGETABLE SALAD

Time: 35 minutes

2 courgettes
1 red pepper
8 vine tomatoes
2 garlic cloves
1 aubergine
handful black olives
1 tbsp white wine vinegar
3 tbsp olive oil
salt and pepper
crumbled feta cheese
handful sundried tomatoes

1. Start by slicing the courgettes lengthways with a potato peeler to make ribbons.

2. Cut the pepper into slithers then dry-fry with courgettes in a pan and when charred, set aside.

3. Preheat the oven to 180°C (gas mark 4) and scatter whole tomatoes and crushed garlic onto a greased baking tray with the courgette and pepper. Slice the aubergine and olives and add.

4. Drizzle with vinegar and oil. Sprinkle with salt and pepper, then place in the oven for 15 minutes until sizzling.

5. Top with the feta cheese and sundried tomatoes.

Fine Dining Steak

Time: 30 minutes

6 new potatoes
4 tbsp olive oil
bunch rosemary
salt and pepper
2 beef steaks
1 garlic clove
spinach salad to serve
small knob butter

1. Chop the potatoes into 2-cm cubes, boil for five minutes, drain and pat dry with a tea towel.

2. Add the potatoes and 2 tbsp of oil to a frying pan and fry for 15 minutes until brown and crispy.

3. When the potatoes look cooked, add chopped rosemary, salt and pepper.

4. Massage the steaks with butter and crushed garlic and fry in 2 tbsp of oil, salt, pepper and chopped rosemary in a hot pan until cooked to your preference.

5. Serve with a spinach salad and enjoy!

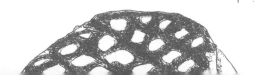

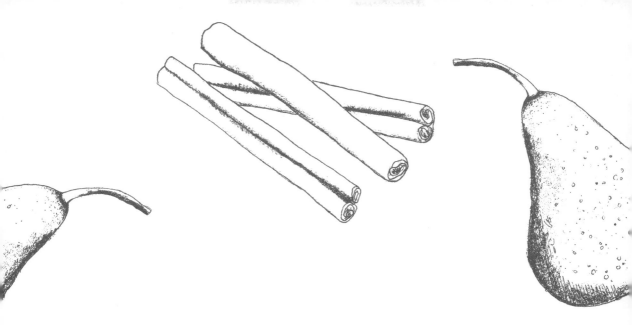

SWEETHEARTS' CARAMEL PEARS

Time: 1 hour

4 pears, peeled
320 g soft brown sugar
4 cardamom pods
2 cinnamon sticks
1 tsp vanilla extract
whipped cream to serve

1. Boil the pears in 1 litre of boiling water. Stir in the sugar, cardamom, cinnamon sticks and vanilla extract.

2. Cook for around 30 minutes then remove the pears and place to one side.

3. Continue to boil the liquid for around 25 minutes until it thickens like honey. Remove the spices.

4. Drizzle the mixture over the pears and serve with whipped cream. Delicious!

SMALL THINGS BECOME
GREAT WHEN DONE WITH LOVE

- Chapter Seven -
Dining in Paris

Parisian jazz, alfresco dining and
these three dishes will make your
night incredible. Accompany with
some French bread, pastries and of
course, a good bottle of French red.

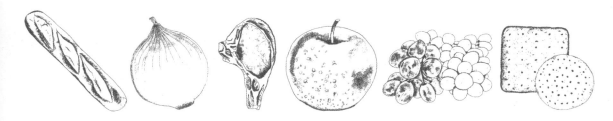

CREAMY FRENCH ONION SOUP

Time: 50 minutes

500 g white onions
2 cloves of garlic
2 tbsp butter
2 tsp honey
1 beef stock cube
1.5 litre water
2 tbsp white wine vinegar
12 ml double cream
salt and pepper
double cream to serve
French bread to serve

1. Dice the onions and finely chop the garlic.

2. Take your largest saucepan and melt the butter. When melted, fry the onions and garlic on a medium heat, for around fifteen minutes, until brown.

3. Add the honey to the mixture and fry gently for another ten minutes, being careful not to burn it.

4. Mix the stock cube into the water and pour into the pan, then simmer for around 15–20 minutes with the lid on.

5. Add the vinegar, cream, salt and pepper to the soup, remove from the heat and whizz with a hand blender on a medium speed until smooth.

6. Reheat and then serve with a swirling of double cream to taste, and French bread. *Voilà!*

Pork Chops
À la Normande

Time: 40 minutes

2 knobs of butter
2 pork chops
300 ml French cidre
salt and pepper
1 Granny Smith apple
8 new potatoes, halved
1 tbsp wholegrain mustard
100 ml double cream
parsley, to serve
fresh salad to serve

1. Melt a large knob of butter in a pan and fry the pork chops over a medium heat, browning them on both sides.

2. Cover the chops in the cidre, salt and pepper and leave for the liquid to reduce.

3. Meanwhile slice the apple thinly and bake in the oven at 180°C (gas mark 4). When browned, set aside.

4. Put the potatoes on to boil on a high heat for around eight minutes until soft.

5. When the cidre has considerably reduced, add the wholegrain mustard and double cream to the chops and boil for about two minutes.

6. Top with parsley and the apples and serve with the potatoes and salad.

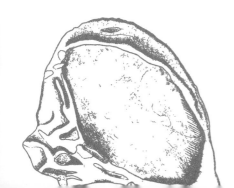

Cheese, Crackers and Red Wine

Time: 5 minutes

1 Camembert or Brie
1 strong Stilton
1 goat's cheese
1 bottle French red wine
a selection of crackers
1 punnet red and
white grapes

1. Place all the cheeses on a cheese board and provide each with its own knife so as not to mix the flavours.

2. Pour very large glasses of red wine and enjoy with crackers and grapes. *C'est fantastique!*

JE T'AIME!

– Chapter Eight –
Movie Marathon

A great early relationship date! Grab these
easy, delicious dishes and some movies
of your choice and get watching.

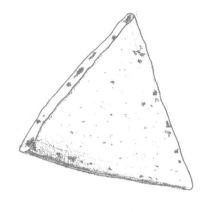

SHARING NACHOS

Time: 15 minutes

1 large packet of tortilla chips
100 g Cheddar cheese
200 g salsa
200 g guacamole
200 g sour cream
pinch of chilli flakes
1 spring onion

1. Scatter out the tortilla chips onto a greased baking tray.

2. Grate the Cheddar cheese evenly over the chips, mixing in with the nachos as you go so the lower layers are coated too.

3. Dot salsa, guacamole and sour cream equally across the chips and top with chilli flakes and the chopped green tops of the spring onion.

4. Preheat the oven to 180°C (gas mark 4) and cook until the cheese is melted and tortillas are browned.

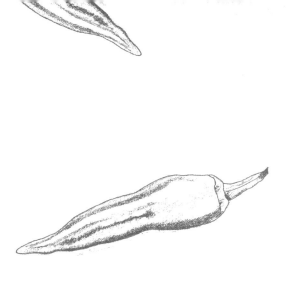
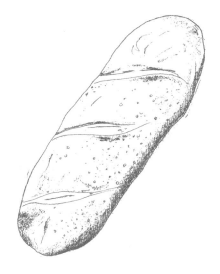

HOME CINEMA HOTDOG

Time: 35 minutes

1 red onion
1 chilli
2 tbsp olive oil
1 tbsp brown sugar
salt and pepper
6 chipolata sausages
3 tbsp wholegrain mustard
2 hot dog rolls
1 pack rocket
1 tbsp tomato puree
coriander
balsamic vinegar

1. Scatter sliced onion and chopped chilli into a roasting dish and season with oil, sugar, salt and pepper.

2. Bake for 15 minutes at 180°C (gas mark 4) until sizzling and brown.

3. Cook the sausages on a separate shelf until well done.

4. Spread the wholegrain mustard liberally inside the hot dog rolls and fill with sausages, rocket, onion and chilli mix, tomato puree and coriander.

5. Drizzle with balsamic vinegar to finish.

Sea Salt Caramel Popcorn

Time: 15 minutes

100 ml Carnation caramel
1 tsp vanilla extract
200 g popped popcorn
1 tsp sea salt
60 g pecan halves
60 g almonds

1. In a saucepan, warm the caramel, stirring continuously.

2. Add the vanilla extract and simmer gently.

3. Drizzle the caramel over the popcorn.

4. Sprinkle with sea salt, pecans and almonds.

You make my heart smile!

- Chapter Nine -
Under The Stars

Grab a blanket, plenty of cushions
and some great food and enjoy the
beautiful outdoors! A clear, starry
night makes this date perfect.

Sweet, Glazed Corn on the Cob

Time: 25 minutes

2 tbsp honey
2 tbsp olive oil
salt and pepper
2–4 large corn on the cob
4 cloves garlic
1 tbsp melted butter
1 lime to serve

1. Prepare the sweet glaze in advance by mixing the honey with the oil. Add a sprinkling of salt and pepper to your taste.

2. Remove the stem and leaves of the corn (if necessary). Then skewer the corn at the base so it's really easy to rotate on the BBQ.

3. Halve the garlic cloves and rub down all sides of the corn.

4. Get the BBQ nice and hot and, when coals are white, place the skewered corn on the BBQ.

5. Rotate until the corn starts to brown all over, then use a spoon to smother over butter and the sweet glaze.

6. Continue to smother and rotate until the corn is a dark golden-brown then serve with thinly sliced lime.

Seafood Paella

Time: 1 hour 10 minutes

100 ml olive oil
1 onion, finely chopped
2 red or yellow peppers,
finely chopped
½ tin chopped tomatoes
1 tin artichoke hearts, washed
2 cloves garlic
large pinch saffron
salt and pepper
250 g paella rice
1 stock cube
1 litre boiling water
4 large tiger prawns
100 g mussels
lemon slices to serve

1. Add the olive oil to a pan and fry the onion and pepper until soft.

2. Pour in the chopped tomatoes, artichokes, garlic, saffron, salt and pepper and stir to combine.

3. When the mixture is soft, add paella rice and stir well, making sure all grains are coated.

4. Mix the stock cube with 1 litre of boiling water in a separate jug and add to the vegetables boiling for 15 minutes.

5. Add the prawns and mussels and cook for another 5 minutes.

6. Turn the heat off completely and cover the pan with a heavy lid or a few tea towels. This needs to remain covered for 20 minutes.

7. When the time's up serve with the lemon!

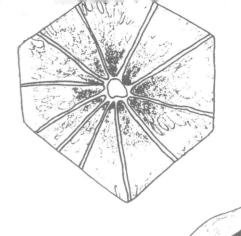

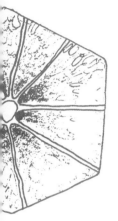

TIPSY ORANGE SALAD

Time: 20 minutes

3–4 large oranges
1 tbsp icing sugar
1 tsp cinnamon
50 ml white rum
Greek yogurt to serve
crushed, shelled pistachios,
to serve

1. This dish can be prepared a couple of hours before your date then brought along in a container.

2. Chop the skin and white bits off the oranges and slice into thin discs.

3. Sprinkle the icing sugar and cinnamon through a sieve all over the oranges and douse in the rum.

4. Serve with Greek yogurt and a sprinkling of crushed pistachios.

I'M WEARING THE SMILE
YOU GAVE ME!

Indoor Tent Night
Date Notes

_____

_____

_____

_____

_____

_____

_____

_____

Breakfast in Bed
Date Notes

_____

_____

_____

_____

_____

_____

_____

_____

PICNIC DATE
Date Notes

_____

_____

_____

_____

_____

_____

_____

_____

_____

Dusk Beach
Date Notes

_____

_____

_____

_____

_____

_____

_____

_____

_____

Afternoon Tea
Date Notes

_____

_____

_____

_____

_____

_____

_____

_____

_____

_____

All Dressed Up, Nowhere to Go
Date Notes

_____

_____

_____

_____

_____

_____

_____

_____

DINING IN PARIS
DATE NOTES

Movie Marathon
Date Notes

_____

_____

_____

_____

_____

_____

_____

_____

Under the Stars
Date Notes

_____

_____

_____

_____

_____

_____

_____

_____

Acknowledgements

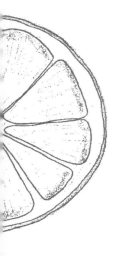

- Massive thanks to the following -

ILLUSTRATIONS AND GRAPHIC DESIGN
Sophie Charnley

GRAPHIC DESIGN
Emma Galvin

- Further thanks to -

Izzie Bergin
Sarah Turner

www.rebeccawarbis.com